MW00720533

THE WINEMAKER'S

RECORD BOOK

A Record Book of Wines Made by

_____

THE WINEMAKER'S

RECORD BOOK

RAINCOAST BOOKS
Vancouver

First published in 1997 by

Raincoast Books
8680 Cambie Street
Vancouver, B.C.
v6p 6m9
(604) 323-7100

1 2 3 4 5 6 7 8 9 10

CANADIAN CATALOGUING IN PUBLICATION DATA

Main entry under title:

The winemaker's record book

ISBN 1-55192-116-2

1. Wine and wine making. 2. Blank-books.
TP548.2.w56 1997   641.8′72   c97-910453-x

Printed and bound in Canada

CONTENTS

INTRODUCTION

Good wine is a necessity of life.

– Thomas Jefferson

Welcome to the world of winemaking. Whether you are new to producing your own wines or an old hand at it, *The Winemaker's Record Book* is intended to be a companion to your winemaking activities. A convenient place to document all of your winemaking successes (and, possibly, some of your flops), this record book will help you to keep track of the many details involved in preparing each batch of wine, including where you make your wine and what grape variety you choose.

The Winemaker's Record Book will heighten your enjoyment of the fruits of your labor by providing a place for you to rate your final product as well as comment on the many tastes and flavors of your wine creations. Winemaking is a labor of love and learning, and because each wine and the conditions under which it is made can vary, this book also serves as a handy reference guide for future batches. Additional space has been provided for you to record your observations on the various wines that you have made, as well as your comments on, for example, what food might complement them or what type of grape to attempt next time.

With space provided to paste in your favorite labels; a section for the addresses and contact numbers of wine shops, fellow winemakers, wine clubs, or friends who just love to imbibe; and a glossary of specialized wine-tasting terms, this book serves as an ideal personal resource for your winemaking endeavors.

Enjoy!

WINEMAKING AND

TASTING NOTES

Wine is earth's answer to the sun.
– Margaret Fuller

Who & Where

WINEMAKING SITE	CO-WINEMAKERS

The Details

WINE / GRAPE VARIETY	$ per BOTTLE
	$ per BATCH
VINTNER / PRODUCER	No. of BOTTLES
	DATE MADE
COUNTRY / REGION	
	DATE BOTTLED
☐ 4-WEEK KIT ☐ 6-WEEK KIT ☐ OTHER_____	

First Tasting (3 months optimum)

DATE	MONTHS after BOTTLING
TASTERS PRESENT	
COMMENTS	

DATE	MONTHS after BOTTLING
TASTERS PRESENT	
COMMENTS	

Second Tasting (6 months optimum)

DATE	MONTHS after BOTTLING
TASTERS PRESENT	
COMMENTS	

Third Tasting (9 months optimum)

GENERAL COMMENTS	
COLOR / APPEARANCE	SWEETNESS
BOUQUET and AROMA	TASTE / ACIDITY
BODY and BALANCE	OVERALL RATING

☐ Plonk ☐ Most Enjoyable

☐ Drinkable ☐ Exceptional

Tasting Notes

Who & Where

WINEMAKING SITE	CO-WINEMAKERS

The Details

WINE / GRAPE VARIETY	$ per BOTTLE
	$ per BATCH
VINTNER / PRODUCER	No. of BOTTLES
	DATE MADE
COUNTRY / REGION	
	DATE BOTTLED
☐ 4-WEEK KIT ☐ 6-WEEK KIT ☐ OTHER_____	

First Tasting (3 months optimum)

DATE	MONTHS after BOTTLING
TASTERS PRESENT	
COMMENTS	

DATE	MONTHS after BOTTLING
TASTERS PRESENT	
COMMENTS	

Second Tasting (6 months optimum)

DATE	MONTHS after BOTTLING
TASTERS PRESENT	
COMMENTS	

Third Tasting (9 months optimum)

GENERAL COMMENTS	
COLOR / APPEARANCE	SWEETNESS
BOUQUET and AROMA	TASTE / ACIDITY
BODY and BALANCE	OVERALL RATING

OVERALL RATING

☐ Plonk ☐ Most Enjoyable

☐ Drinkable ☐ Exceptional

Tasting Notes

Who & Where

WINEMAKING SITE	CO-WINEMAKERS

The Details

WINE / GRAPE VARIETY	$ per BOTTLE
	$ per BATCH
VINTNER / PRODUCER	No. of BOTTLES
	DATE MADE
COUNTRY / REGION	
	DATE BOTTLED
☐ 4-WEEK KIT ☐ 6-WEEK KIT ☐ OTHER_____	

First Tasting (3 months optimum)

DATE	MONTHS after BOTTLING
TASTERS PRESENT	
COMMENTS	

16

DATE	MONTHS after BOTTLING
TASTERS PRESENT	
COMMENTS	

Second Tasting (*6 months optimum*)

DATE	MONTHS after BOTTLING
TASTERS PRESENT	
COMMENTS	

Third Tasting (*9 months optimum*)

GENERAL COMMENTS	
COLOR / APPEARANCE	SWEETNESS
BOUQUET and AROMA	TASTE / ACIDITY
BODY and BALANCE	OVERALL RATING ☐ *Plonk*　　☐ *Most Enjoyable* ☐ *Drinkable*　　☐ *Exceptional*

Tasting Notes

Who & Where

WINEMAKING SITE	CO-WINEMAKERS

The Details

WINE / GRAPE VARIETY	$ per BOTTLE
	$ per BATCH
VINTNER / PRODUCER	No. of BOTTLES
	DATE MADE
COUNTRY / REGION	
	DATE BOTTLED
☐ 4-WEEK KIT ☐ 6-WEEK KIT ☐ OTHER_____	

First Tasting (3 months optimum)

DATE	MONTHS after BOTTLING
TASTERS PRESENT	
COMMENTS	

DATE	MONTHS after BOTTLING
TASTERS PRESENT	
COMMENTS	

Second Tasting (6 months optimum)

DATE	MONTHS after BOTTLING
TASTERS PRESENT	
COMMENTS	

Third Tasting (9 months optimum)

GENERAL COMMENTS	
COLOR / APPEARANCE	SWEETNESS
BOUQUET and AROMA	TASTE / ACIDITY
BODY and BALANCE	OVERALL RATING ☐ Plonk ☐ Most Enjoyable ☐ Drinkable ☐ Exceptional

Tasting Notes

Who & Where

WINEMAKING SITE	CO-WINEMAKERS

The Details

WINE / GRAPE VARIETY	$ per BOTTLE
	$ per BATCH
VINTNER / PRODUCER	No. of BOTTLES
	DATE MADE
COUNTRY / REGION	
	DATE BOTTLED
☐ 4-WEEK KIT　　☐ 6-WEEK KIT　　☐ OTHER_____	

First Tasting (3 months optimum)

DATE	MONTHS after BOTTLING
TASTERS PRESENT	
COMMENTS	

DATE	MONTHS after BOTTLING
TASTERS PRESENT	
COMMENTS	

Second Tasting (6 months optimum)

DATE	MONTHS after BOTTLING
TASTERS PRESENT	
COMMENTS	

Third Tasting (9 months optimum)

GENERAL COMMENTS	
COLOR / APPEARANCE	SWEETNESS
BOUQUET and AROMA	TASTE / ACIDITY
BODY and BALANCE	OVERALL RATING ☐ Plonk ☐ Most Enjoyable ☐ Drinkable ☐ Exceptional

Tasting Notes

Who & Where

WINEMAKING SITE	CO-WINEMAKERS

The Details

WINE / GRAPE VARIETY	$ per BOTTLE
	$ per BATCH
VINTNER / PRODUCER	No. of BOTTLES
	DATE MADE
COUNTRY / REGION	
	DATE BOTTLED
☐ 4-WEEK KIT ☐ 6-WEEK KIT ☐ OTHER_____	

First Tasting (3 months optimum)

DATE	MONTHS after BOTTLING
TASTERS PRESENT	
COMMENTS	

DATE	MONTHS after BOTTLING
TASTERS PRESENT	
COMMENTS	

Second Tasting (6 months optimum)

DATE	MONTHS after BOTTLING
TASTERS PRESENT	
COMMENTS	

Third Tasting (9 months optimum)

GENERAL COMMENTS	
COLOR / APPEARANCE	SWEETNESS
BOUQUET and AROMA	TASTE / ACIDITY
BODY and BALANCE	OVERALL RATING

OVERALL RATING

☐ Plonk   ☐ Most Enjoyable

☐ Drinkable   ☐ Exceptional

Tasting Notes

Who & Where

WINEMAKING SITE	CO-WINEMAKERS

The Details

WINE / GRAPE VARIETY	$ per BOTTLE
	$ per BATCH
VINTNER / PRODUCER	No. of BOTTLES
	DATE MADE
COUNTRY / REGION	
	DATE BOTTLED

☐ 4-WEEK KIT ☐ 6-WEEK KIT ☐ OTHER_____

First Tasting (3 months optimum)

DATE	MONTHS after BOTTLING
TASTERS PRESENT	

COMMENTS

DATE	MONTHS after BOTTLING
TASTERS PRESENT	
COMMENTS	

Second Tasting (6 months optimum)

DATE	MONTHS after BOTTLING
TASTERS PRESENT	
COMMENTS	

Third Tasting (9 months optimum)

GENERAL COMMENTS	
COLOR / APPEARANCE	SWEETNESS
BOUQUET and AROMA	TASTE / ACIDITY
BODY and BALANCE	OVERALL RATING ☐ Plonk ☐ Most Enjoyable ☐ Drinkable ☐ Exceptional

Tasting Notes

Who & Where

WINEMAKING SITE	CO-WINEMAKERS

The Details

WINE / GRAPE VARIETY	$ per BOTTLE
	$ per BATCH
VINTNER / PRODUCER	No. of BOTTLES
	DATE MADE
COUNTRY / REGION	
	DATE BOTTLED
☐ 4-WEEK KIT ☐ 6-WEEK KIT ☐ OTHER_____	

First Tasting (3 months optimum)

DATE	MONTHS after BOTTLING
TASTERS PRESENT	
COMMENTS	

DATE	MONTHS after BOTTLING
TASTERS PRESENT	
COMMENTS	

Second Tasting (6 months optimum)

DATE	MONTHS after BOTTLING
TASTERS PRESENT	
COMMENTS	

Third Tasting (9 months optimum)

GENERAL COMMENTS	
COLOR / APPEARANCE	SWEETNESS
BOUQUET and AROMA	TASTE / ACIDITY
BODY and BALANCE	OVERALL RATING

OVERALL RATING

☐ Plonk ☐ Most Enjoyable

☐ Drinkable ☐ Exceptional

Tasting Notes

Who & Where

WINEMAKING SITE	CO-WINEMAKERS

The Details

WINE / GRAPE VARIETY	$ per BOTTLE
	$ per BATCH
VINTNER / PRODUCER	No. of BOTTLES
	DATE MADE
COUNTRY / REGION	
	DATE BOTTLED
☐ 4-WEEK KIT ☐ 6-WEEK KIT ☐ OTHER _____	

First Tasting (3 months optimum)

DATE	MONTHS after BOTTLING
TASTERS PRESENT	
COMMENTS	

DATE	MONTHS after BOTTLING
TASTERS PRESENT	
COMMENTS	

Second Tasting (6 months optimum)

DATE	MONTHS after BOTTLING
TASTERS PRESENT	
COMMENTS	

Third Tasting (9 months optimum)

GENERAL COMMENTS	
COLOR / APPEARANCE	SWEETNESS
BOUQUET and AROMA	TASTE / ACIDITY
BODY and BALANCE	OVERALL RATING
	☐ Plonk ☐ Most Enjoyable
	☐ Drinkable ☐ Exceptional

Tasting Notes

Who & Where

WINEMAKING SITE	CO-WINEMAKERS

The Details

WINE / GRAPE VARIETY	$ per BOTTLE
	$ per BATCH
VINTNER / PRODUCER	No. of BOTTLES
	DATE MADE
COUNTRY / REGION	
	DATE BOTTLED
☐ 4-WEEK KIT ☐ 6-WEEK KIT ☐ OTHER_____	

First Tasting (3 months optimum)

DATE	MONTHS after BOTTLING
TASTERS PRESENT	
COMMENTS	

DATE	MONTHS after BOTTLING
TASTERS PRESENT	
COMMENTS	

Second Tasting (6 months optimum)

DATE	MONTHS after BOTTLING
TASTERS PRESENT	
COMMENTS	

Third Tasting (9 months optimum)

GENERAL COMMENTS	
COLOR / APPEARANCE	SWEETNESS
BOUQUET and AROMA	TASTE / ACIDITY
BODY and BALANCE	OVERALL RATING

OVERALL RATING
☐ *Plonk*   ☐ *Most Enjoyable*
☐ *Drinkable*   ☐ *Exceptional*

Tasting Notes

Who & Where

WINEMAKING SITE	CO-WINEMAKERS

The Details

WINE / GRAPE VARIETY	$ per BOTTLE
	$ per BATCH
VINTNER / PRODUCER	No. of BOTTLES
	DATE MADE
COUNTRY / REGION	
	DATE BOTTLED
☐ 4-WEEK KIT ☐ 6-WEEK KIT ☐ OTHER_____	

First Tasting (3 months optimum)

DATE	MONTHS after BOTTLING
TASTERS PRESENT	
COMMENTS	

DATE	MONTHS after BOTTLING
TASTERS PRESENT	
COMMENTS	

DATE	MONTHS after BOTTLING
TASTERS PRESENT	
COMMENTS	

GENERAL COMMENTS	
COLOR / APPEARANCE	SWEETNESS
BOUQUET and AROMA	TASTE / ACIDITY
BODY and BALANCE	OVERALL RATING

OVERALL RATING

☐ Plonk　　☐ Most Enjoyable

☐ Drinkable　　☐ Exceptional

Who & Where

WINEMAKING SITE	CO-WINEMAKERS

The Details

WINE / GRAPE VARIETY	$ per BOTTLE
	$ per BATCH
VINTNER / PRODUCER	No. of BOTTLES
	DATE MADE
COUNTRY / REGION	
	DATE BOTTLED
☐ 4-WEEK KIT ☐ 6-WEEK KIT ☐ OTHER_____	

First Tasting (3 months optimum)

DATE	MONTHS after BOTTLING
TASTERS PRESENT	
COMMENTS	

DATE	MONTHS after BOTTLING
TASTERS PRESENT	
COMMENTS	

Second Tasting (6 months optimum)

DATE	MONTHS after BOTTLING
TASTERS PRESENT	
COMMENTS	

Third Tasting (9 months optimum)

GENERAL COMMENTS	
COLOR / APPEARANCE	SWEETNESS
BOUQUET and AROMA	TASTE / ACIDITY
BODY and BALANCE	OVERALL RATING

OVERALL RATING

☐ Plonk   ☐ Most Enjoyable

☐ Drinkable   ☐ Exceptional

Tasting Notes

Who & Where

WINEMAKING SITE	CO-WINEMAKERS

The Details

WINE / GRAPE VARIETY	$ per BOTTLE
	$ per BATCH
VINTNER / PRODUCER	No. of BOTTLES
	DATE MADE
COUNTRY / REGION	
	DATE BOTTLED
☐ 4-WEEK KIT ☐ 6-WEEK KIT ☐ OTHER_____	

First Tasting (3 months optimum)

DATE	MONTHS after BOTTLING
TASTERS PRESENT	
COMMENTS	

DATE	MONTHS after BOTTLING
TASTERS PRESENT	
COMMENTS	

Second Tasting (6 months optimum)

DATE	MONTHS after BOTTLING
TASTERS PRESENT	
COMMENTS	

Third Tasting (9 months optimum)

GENERAL COMMENTS	
COLOR / APPEARANCE	SWEETNESS
BOUQUET and AROMA	TASTE / ACIDITY
BODY and BALANCE	OVERALL RATING

OVERALL RATING

☐ Plonk   ☐ Most Enjoyable

☐ Drinkable   ☐ Exceptional

Tasting Notes

Who & Where

WINEMAKING SITE	CO-WINEMAKERS

The Details

WINE / GRAPE VARIETY	$ per BOTTLE
	$ per BATCH
VINTNER / PRODUCER	No. of BOTTLES
	DATE MADE
COUNTRY / REGION	
	DATE BOTTLED
☐ 4-WEEK KIT ☐ 6-WEEK KIT ☐ OTHER_____	

First Tasting (*3 months optimum*)

DATE	MONTHS after BOTTLING
TASTERS PRESENT	
COMMENTS	

DATE	MONTHS after BOTTLING
TASTERS PRESENT	
COMMENTS	

Second Tasting (6 months optimum)

DATE	MONTHS after BOTTLING
TASTERS PRESENT	
COMMENTS	

Third Tasting (9 months optimum)

GENERAL COMMENTS	
COLOR / APPEARANCE	SWEETNESS
BOUQUET and AROMA	TASTE / ACIDITY
BODY and BALANCE	OVERALL RATING

OVERALL RATING
☐ Plonk   ☐ Most Enjoyable
☐ Drinkable   ☐ Exceptional

Tasting Notes

Who & Where

WINEMAKING SITE	CO-WINEMAKERS

The Details

WINE / GRAPE VARIETY	$ per BOTTLE
	$ per BATCH
VINTNER / PRODUCER	No. of BOTTLES
	DATE MADE
COUNTRY / REGION	
	DATE BOTTLED
☐ 4-WEEK KIT ☐ 6-WEEK KIT ☐ OTHER_____	

First Tasting (3 months optimum)

DATE	MONTHS after BOTTLING
TASTERS PRESENT	
COMMENTS	

DATE	MONTHS after BOTTLING
TASTERS PRESENT	
COMMENTS	

Second Tasting (*6 months optimum*)

DATE	MONTHS after BOTTLING
TASTERS PRESENT	
COMMENTS	

Third Tasting (*9 months optimum*)

GENERAL COMMENTS	
COLOR / APPEARANCE	SWEETNESS
BOUQUET and AROMA	TASTE / ACIDITY
BODY and BALANCE	OVERALL RATING

OVERALL RATING

☐ Plonk ☐ Most Enjoyable

☐ Drinkable ☐ Exceptional

Tasting Notes

Who & Where

WINEMAKING SITE	CO-WINEMAKERS

The Details

WINE / GRAPE VARIETY	$ per BOTTLE
	$ per BATCH
VINTNER / PRODUCER	No. of BOTTLES
	DATE MADE
COUNTRY / REGION	
	DATE BOTTLED

☐ 4-WEEK KIT   ☐ 6-WEEK KIT   ☐ OTHER_____

First Tasting (3 months optimum)

DATE	MONTHS after BOTTLING
TASTERS PRESENT	

COMMENTS

DATE	MONTHS after BOTTLING
TASTERS PRESENT	
COMMENTS	

Second Tasting (6 months optimum)

DATE	MONTHS after BOTTLING
TASTERS PRESENT	
COMMENTS	

Third Tasting (9 months optimum)

GENERAL COMMENTS	
COLOR / APPEARANCE	SWEETNESS
BOUQUET and AROMA	TASTE / ACIDITY
BODY and BALANCE	OVERALL RATING

OVERALL RATING

☐ *Plonk*   ☐ *Most Enjoyable*

☐ *Drinkable*   ☐ *Exceptional*

Tasting Notes

Who & Where

WINEMAKING SITE	CO-WINEMAKERS

The Details

WINE / GRAPE VARIETY	$ per BOTTLE
	$ per BATCH
VINTNER / PRODUCER	No. of BOTTLES
	DATE MADE
COUNTRY / REGION	
	DATE BOTTLED
☐ 4-WEEK KIT ☐ 6-WEEK KIT ☐ OTHER_____	

First Tasting (3 months optimum)

DATE	MONTHS after BOTTLING
TASTERS PRESENT	
COMMENTS	

44

DATE	MONTHS after BOTTLING
TASTERS PRESENT	
COMMENTS	

Second Tasting (6 months optimum)

DATE	MONTHS after BOTTLING
TASTERS PRESENT	
COMMENTS	

Third Tasting (9 months optimum)

GENERAL COMMENTS	
COLOR / APPEARANCE	SWEETNESS
BOUQUET and AROMA	TASTE / ACIDITY
BODY and BALANCE	OVERALL RATING

OVERALL RATING
- ☐ Plonk
- ☐ Drinkable
- ☐ Most Enjoyable
- ☐ Exceptional

Tasting Notes

Who & Where

WINEMAKING SITE	CO-WINEMAKERS

The Details

WINE / GRAPE VARIETY	$ per BOTTLE
	$ per BATCH
VINTNER / PRODUCER	No. of BOTTLES
	DATE MADE
COUNTRY / REGION	
	DATE BOTTLED
☐ 4-WEEK KIT ☐ 6-WEEK KIT ☐ OTHER_____	

First Tasting (3 months optimum)

DATE	MONTHS after BOTTLING
TASTERS PRESENT	
COMMENTS	

DATE	MONTHS after BOTTLING
TASTERS PRESENT	
COMMENTS	

Second Tasting (6 months optimum)

DATE	MONTHS after BOTTLING
TASTERS PRESENT	
COMMENTS	

Third Tasting (9 months optimum)

GENERAL COMMENTS	
COLOR / APPEARANCE	SWEETNESS
BOUQUET and AROMA	TASTE / ACIDITY
BODY and BALANCE	OVERALL RATING

OVERALL RATING

☐ *Plonk*   ☐ *Most Enjoyable*

☐ *Drinkable*   ☐ *Exceptional*

Tasting Notes

Who & Where

WINEMAKING SITE	CO-WINEMAKERS

The Details

WINE / GRAPE VARIETY	$ per BOTTLE
	$ per BATCH
VINTNER / PRODUCER	No. of BOTTLES
	DATE MADE
COUNTRY / REGION	
	DATE BOTTLED
☐ 4-WEEK KIT ☐ 6-WEEK KIT ☐ OTHER_____	

First Tasting (*3 months optimum*)

DATE	MONTHS after BOTTLING
TASTERS PRESENT	
COMMENTS	

DATE	MONTHS after BOTTLING	
TASTERS PRESENT		
COMMENTS		

Second Tasting (6 months optimum)

DATE	MONTHS after BOTTLING	
TASTERS PRESENT		
COMMENTS		

Third Tasting (9 months optimum)

GENERAL COMMENTS		
COLOR / APPEARANCE	SWEETNESS	
BOUQUET and AROMA	TASTE / ACIDITY	
BODY and BALANCE	OVERALL RATING	
	☐ Plonk ☐ Most Enjoyable	
	☐ Drinkable ☐ Exceptional	

Tasting Notes

Who & Where

WINEMAKING SITE	CO-WINEMAKERS

The Details

WINE / GRAPE VARIETY	$ per BOTTLE
	$ per BATCH
VINTNER / PRODUCER	No. of BOTTLES
	DATE MADE
COUNTRY / REGION	
	DATE BOTTLED
☐ 4-WEEK KIT ☐ 6-WEEK KIT ☐ OTHER_____	

First Tasting (3 months optimum)

DATE	MONTHS after BOTTLING
TASTERS PRESENT	
COMMENTS	

DATE	MONTHS after BOTTLING
TASTERS PRESENT	
COMMENTS	

Second Tasting (6 months optimum)

DATE	MONTHS after BOTTLING
TASTERS PRESENT	
COMMENTS	

Third Tasting (9 months optimum)

GENERAL COMMENTS	
COLOR / APPEARANCE	SWEETNESS
BOUQUET and AROMA	TASTE / ACIDITY
BODY and BALANCE	OVERALL RATING

OVERALL RATING

☐ Plonk ☐ Most Enjoyable

☐ Drinkable ☐ Exceptional

Tasting Notes

Who & Where

WINEMAKING SITE	CO-WINEMAKERS

The Details

WINE / GRAPE VARIETY	$ per BOTTLE
	$ per BATCH
VINTNER / PRODUCER	No. of BOTTLES
	DATE MADE
COUNTRY / REGION	
	DATE BOTTLED

☐ 4-WEEK KIT   ☐ 6-WEEK KIT   ☐ OTHER_____

First Tasting (3 months optimum)

DATE	MONTHS after BOTTLING
TASTERS PRESENT	
COMMENTS	

DATE	MONTHS after BOTTLING
TASTERS PRESENT	
COMMENTS	

Second Tasting (6 months optimum)

DATE	MONTHS after BOTTLING
TASTERS PRESENT	
COMMENTS	

Third Tasting (9 months optimum)

GENERAL COMMENTS	
COLOR / APPEARANCE	SWEETNESS
BOUQUET and AROMA	TASTE / ACIDITY
BODY and BALANCE	OVERALL RATING

OVERALL RATING
☐ Plonk   ☐ Most Enjoyable
☐ Drinkable   ☐ Exceptional

Tasting Notes

53

Who & Where

WINEMAKING SITE	CO-WINEMAKERS

The Details

WINE / GRAPE VARIETY	$ per BOTTLE
	$ per BATCH
VINTNER / PRODUCER	No. of BOTTLES
	DATE MADE
COUNTRY / REGION	
	DATE BOTTLED
☐ 4-WEEK KIT ☐ 6-WEEK KIT ☐ OTHER_____	

First Tasting (3 months optimum)

DATE	MONTHS after BOTTLING
TASTERS PRESENT	
COMMENTS	

DATE	MONTHS after BOTTLING
TASTERS PRESENT	
COMMENTS	

Second Tasting (6 months optimum)

DATE	MONTHS after BOTTLING
TASTERS PRESENT	
COMMENTS	

Third Tasting (9 months optimum)

GENERAL COMMENTS	
COLOR / APPEARANCE	SWEETNESS
BOUQUET and AROMA	TASTE / ACIDITY
BODY and BALANCE	OVERALL RATING

OVERALL RATING

☐ Plonk   ☐ Most Enjoyable

☐ Drinkable   ☐ Exceptional

Tasting Notes

Who & Where

WINEMAKING SITE	CO-WINEMAKERS

The Details

WINE / GRAPE VARIETY	$ per BOTTLE
	$ per BATCH
VINTNER / PRODUCER	No. of BOTTLES
	DATE MADE
COUNTRY / REGION	
	DATE BOTTLED
☐ 4-WEEK KIT ☐ 6-WEEK KIT ☐ OTHER_____	

First Tasting (3 months optimum)

DATE	MONTHS after BOTTLING
TASTERS PRESENT	
COMMENTS	

DATE	MONTHS after BOTTLING
TASTERS PRESENT	
COMMENTS	

Second Tasting (*6 months optimum*)

DATE	MONTHS after BOTTLING
TASTERS PRESENT	
COMMENTS	

Third Tasting (*9 months optimum*)

GENERAL COMMENTS	
COLOR / APPEARANCE	SWEETNESS
BOUQUET and AROMA	TASTE / ACIDITY
BODY and BALANCE	OVERALL RATING

OVERALL RATING

☐ *Plonk*   ☐ *Most Enjoyable*

☐ *Drinkable*   ☐ *Exceptional*

Tasting Notes

Who & Where

WINEMAKING SITE	CO-WINEMAKERS

The Details

WINE / GRAPE VARIETY	$ per BOTTLE
	$ per BATCH
VINTNER / PRODUCER	No. of BOTTLES
	DATE MADE
COUNTRY / REGION	
	DATE BOTTLED
☐ 4-WEEK KIT　　☐ 6-WEEK KIT　　☐ OTHER_____	

First Tasting (3 months optimum)

DATE	MONTHS after BOTTLING
TASTERS PRESENT	
COMMENTS	

DATE	MONTHS after BOTTLING

TASTERS PRESENT

COMMENTS

Second Tasting (6 months optimum)

DATE	MONTHS after BOTTLING

TASTERS PRESENT

COMMENTS

Third Tasting (9 months optimum)

GENERAL COMMENTS

COLOR / APPEARANCE	SWEETNESS

BOUQUET and AROMA	TASTE / ACIDITY

BODY and BALANCE	OVERALL RATING
	☐ Plonk ☐ Most Enjoyable
	☐ Drinkable ☐ Exceptional

Tasting Notes

59

Who & Where

WINEMAKING SITE	CO-WINEMAKERS

The Details

WINE / GRAPE VARIETY	$ per BOTTLE
	$ per BATCH
VINTNER / PRODUCER	No. of BOTTLES
	DATE MADE
COUNTRY / REGION	
	DATE BOTTLED
☐ 4-WEEK KIT ☐ 6-WEEK KIT ☐ OTHER_____	

First Tasting (3 months optimum)

DATE	MONTHS after BOTTLING
TASTERS PRESENT	
COMMENTS	

DATE	MONTHS after BOTTLING
TASTERS PRESENT	
COMMENTS	

Second Tasting (6 months optimum)

DATE	MONTHS after BOTTLING
TASTERS PRESENT	
COMMENTS	

Third Tasting (9 months optimum)

GENERAL COMMENTS	
COLOR / APPEARANCE	SWEETNESS
BOUQUET and AROMA	TASTE / ACIDITY
BODY and BALANCE	OVERALL RATING ☐ Plonk ☐ Most Enjoyable ☐ Drinkable ☐ Exceptional

Tasting Notes

Who & Where

WINEMAKING SITE	CO-WINEMAKERS

The Details

WINE / GRAPE VARIETY	$ per BOTTLE
	$ per BATCH
VINTNER / PRODUCER	No. of BOTTLES
	DATE MADE
COUNTRY / REGION	
	DATE BOTTLED
☐ 4-WEEK KIT ☐ 6-WEEK KIT ☐ OTHER_____	

First Tasting (3 months optimum)

DATE	MONTHS after BOTTLING
TASTERS PRESENT	
COMMENTS	

62

DATE	MONTHS after BOTTLING
TASTERS PRESENT	
COMMENTS	

Second Tasting (*6 months optimum*)

DATE	MONTHS after BOTTLING
TASTERS PRESENT	
COMMENTS	

Third Tasting (*9 months optimum*)

GENERAL COMMENTS	
COLOR / APPEARANCE	SWEETNESS
BOUQUET and AROMA	TASTE / ACIDITY
BODY and BALANCE	OVERALL RATING

OVERALL RATING

☐ *Plonk*   ☐ *Most Enjoyable*

☐ *Drinkable*   ☐ *Exceptional*

Tasting Notes

Who & Where

WINEMAKING SITE	CO-WINEMAKERS

The Details

WINE / GRAPE VARIETY	$ per BOTTLE
	$ per BATCH
VINTNER / PRODUCER	No. of BOTTLES
	DATE MADE
COUNTRY / REGION	
	DATE BOTTLED
☐ 4-WEEK KIT ☐ 6-WEEK KIT ☐ OTHER_____	

First Tasting (*3 months optimum*)

DATE	MONTHS after BOTTLING
TASTERS PRESENT	
COMMENTS	

DATE	MONTHS after BOTTLING
TASTERS PRESENT	
COMMENTS	

Second Tasting (6 months optimum)

DATE	MONTHS after BOTTLING
TASTERS PRESENT	
COMMENTS	

Third Tasting (9 months optimum)

GENERAL COMMENTS	
COLOR / APPEARANCE	SWEETNESS
BOUQUET and AROMA	TASTE / ACIDITY
BODY and BALANCE	OVERALL RATING ☐ Plonk ☐ Most Enjoyable ☐ Drinkable ☐ Exceptional

Tasting Notes

Who & Where

WINEMAKING SITE	CO-WINEMAKERS

The Details

WINE / GRAPE VARIETY	$ per BOTTLE
	$ per BATCH
VINTNER / PRODUCER	No. of BOTTLES
	DATE MADE
COUNTRY / REGION	
	DATE BOTTLED

☐ 4-WEEK KIT ☐ 6-WEEK KIT ☐ OTHER_____

First Tasting (3 months optimum)

DATE	MONTHS after BOTTLING
TASTERS PRESENT	
COMMENTS	

66

DATE	MONTHS after BOTTLING
TASTERS PRESENT	
COMMENTS	

Second Tasting (6 months optimum)

DATE	MONTHS after BOTTLING
TASTERS PRESENT	
COMMENTS	

Third Tasting (9 months optimum)

GENERAL COMMENTS	
COLOR / APPEARANCE	SWEETNESS
BOUQUET and AROMA	TASTE / ACIDITY
BODY and BALANCE	OVERALL RATING ☐ Plonk ☐ Most Enjoyable ☐ Drinkable ☐ Exceptional

Tasting Notes

Who & Where

WINEMAKING SITE	CO-WINEMAKERS

The Details

WINE / GRAPE VARIETY	$ per BOTTLE
	$ per BATCH
VINTNER / PRODUCER	No. of BOTTLES
	DATE MADE
COUNTRY / REGION	
	DATE BOTTLED
☐ 4-WEEK KIT ☐ 6-WEEK KIT ☐ OTHER_____	

First Tasting (3 months optimum)

DATE	MONTHS after BOTTLING
TASTERS PRESENT	
COMMENTS	

DATE	MONTHS after BOTTLING
TASTERS PRESENT	
COMMENTS	

Second Tasting (6 months optimum)

DATE	MONTHS after BOTTLING
TASTERS PRESENT	
COMMENTS	

Third Tasting (9 months optimum)

GENERAL COMMENTS	
COLOR / APPEARANCE	SWEETNESS
BOUQUET and AROMA	TASTE / ACIDITY
BODY and BALANCE	OVERALL RATING

OVERALL RATING

☐ Plonk   ☐ Most Enjoyable

☐ Drinkable   ☐ Exceptional

Tasting Notes

Who & Where

WINEMAKING SITE	CO-WINEMAKERS

The Details

WINE / GRAPE VARIETY	$ per BOTTLE
	$ per BATCH
VINTNER / PRODUCER	No. of BOTTLES
	DATE MADE
COUNTRY / REGION	
	DATE BOTTLED
☐ 4-WEEK KIT ☐ 6-WEEK KIT ☐ OTHER_____	

First Tasting (3 months optimum)

DATE	MONTHS after BOTTLING
TASTERS PRESENT	
COMMENTS	

DATE	MONTHS after BOTTLING
TASTERS PRESENT	
COMMENTS	

Second Tasting (*6 months optimum*)

DATE	MONTHS after BOTTLING
TASTERS PRESENT	
COMMENTS	

Third Tasting (*9 months optimum*)

GENERAL COMMENTS	
COLOR / APPEARANCE	SWEETNESS
BOUQUET and AROMA	TASTE / ACIDITY
BODY and BALANCE	OVERALL RATING ☐ Plonk ☐ Most Enjoyable ☐ Drinkable ☐ Exceptional

Tasting Notes

Who & Where

WINEMAKING SITE	CO-WINEMAKERS

The Details

WINE / GRAPE VARIETY	$ per BOTTLE
	$ per BATCH
VINTNER / PRODUCER	No. of BOTTLES
	DATE MADE
COUNTRY / REGION	
	DATE BOTTLED
☐ 4-WEEK KIT　　☐ 6-WEEK KIT　　☐ OTHER_____	

First Tasting (3 months optimum)

DATE	MONTHS after BOTTLING
TASTERS PRESENT	
COMMENTS	

DATE	MONTHS after BOTTLING
TASTERS PRESENT	
COMMENTS	

Second Tasting (6 months optimum)

DATE	MONTHS after BOTTLING
TASTERS PRESENT	
COMMENTS	

Third Tasting (9 months optimum)

GENERAL COMMENTS	
COLOR / APPEARANCE	SWEETNESS
BOUQUET and AROMA	TASTE / ACIDITY
BODY and BALANCE	OVERALL RATING

OVERALL RATING
☐ Plonk   ☐ Most Enjoyable
☐ Drinkable   ☐ Exceptional

Tasting Notes

THE WINEMAKER'S RECORD BOOK

Who & Where

WINEMAKING SITE	CO-WINEMAKERS

The Details

WINE / GRAPE VARIETY	$ per BOTTLE
	$ per BATCH
VINTNER / PRODUCER	No. of BOTTLES
	DATE MADE
COUNTRY / REGION	
	DATE BOTTLED
☐ 4-WEEK KIT ☐ 6-WEEK KIT ☐ OTHER_____	

First Tasting (3 months optimum)

DATE	MONTHS after BOTTLING
TASTERS PRESENT	
COMMENTS	

DATE	MONTHS after BOTTLING
TASTERS PRESENT	
COMMENTS	

Second Tasting (6 months optimum)

DATE	MONTHS after BOTTLING
TASTERS PRESENT	
COMMENTS	

Third Tasting (9 months optimum)

GENERAL COMMENTS	
COLOR / APPEARANCE	SWEETNESS
BOUQUET and AROMA	TASTE / ACIDITY
BODY and BALANCE	OVERALL RATING

OVERALL RATING

☐ *Plonk* ☐ *Most Enjoyable*

☐ *Drinkable* ☐ *Exceptional*

Tasting Notes

Who & Where

WINEMAKING SITE	CO-WINEMAKERS

The Details

WINE / GRAPE VARIETY	$ per BOTTLE
	$ per BATCH
VINTNER / PRODUCER	No. of BOTTLES
	DATE MADE
COUNTRY / REGION	
	DATE BOTTLED
☐ 4-WEEK KIT ☐ 6-WEEK KIT ☐ OTHER_____	

First Tasting (3 *months* optimum)

DATE	MONTHS after BOTTLING
TASTERS PRESENT	
COMMENTS	

DATE	MONTHS after BOTTLING
TASTERS PRESENT	
COMMENTS	

DATE	MONTHS after BOTTLING
TASTERS PRESENT	
COMMENTS	

GENERAL COMMENTS	
COLOR / APPEARANCE	SWEETNESS
BOUQUET and AROMA	TASTE / ACIDITY
BODY and BALANCE	OVERALL RATING ☐ Plonk ☐ Most Enjoyable ☐ Drinkable ☐ Exceptional

Who & Where

WINEMAKING SITE	CO-WINEMAKERS

The Details

WINE / GRAPE VARIETY	$ per BOTTLE
	$ per BATCH
VINTNER / PRODUCER	No. of BOTTLES
	DATE MADE
COUNTRY / REGION	
	DATE BOTTLED
☐ 4-WEEK KIT ☐ 6-WEEK KIT ☐ OTHER_____	

First Tasting (3 months optimum)

DATE	MONTHS after BOTTLING
TASTERS PRESENT	
COMMENTS	

DATE	MONTHS after BOTTLING
TASTERS PRESENT	
COMMENTS	

Second Tasting (6 months optimum)

DATE	MONTHS after BOTTLING
TASTERS PRESENT	
COMMENTS	

Third Tasting (9 months optimum)

GENERAL COMMENTS	
COLOR / APPEARANCE	SWEETNESS
BOUQUET and AROMA	TASTE / ACIDITY
BODY and BALANCE	OVERALL RATING

OVERALL RATING

☐ Plonk ☐ Most Enjoyable

☐ Drinkable ☐ Exceptional

Tasting Notes

NAME

ADDRESS

PHONE | FAX

NAME

ADDRESS

PHONE | FAX

NAME

ADDRESS

PHONE | FAX

NAME

ADDRESS

PHONE | FAX

NAME

ADDRESS

PHONE | FAX

NAME

ADDRESS

PHONE	FAX

NAME

ADDRESS

PHONE	FAX

NAME

ADDRESS

PHONE	FAX

NAME

ADDRESS

PHONE	FAX

NAME

ADDRESS

PHONE	FAX

NAME	
ADDRESS	
PHONE	FAX

NAME	
ADDRESS	
PHONE	FAX

NAME	
ADDRESS	
PHONE	FAX

NAME	
ADDRESS	
PHONE	FAX

NAME	
ADDRESS	
PHONE	FAX

NAME	
ADDRESS	
PHONE	FAX

NAME	
ADDRESS	
PHONE	FAX

NAME	
ADDRESS	
PHONE	FAX

NAME	
ADDRESS	
PHONE	FAX

NAME	
ADDRESS	
PHONE	FAX

WINE-TASTING TERMS

It is better to have bread left over than to run short of wine.

— Spanish proverb

ACIDITY: The fresh, tart, or sour taste resulting from the amount of natural acid in a wine.

AROMA: The simple, pleasant scent of a young wine.

BALANCE: The relationship between a wine's key elements – alcohol content, flavors, acidity, etc.

BIG: A wine that is full-bodied and flavorful.

BODY: The perceived weight or fullness of a wine in your mouth.

BOUQUET: The varied, complex scent of a mature wine.

CORKY: An inferior bottle of wine – often with a musty, cardboard-like smell – resulting from a bad cork.

CRISP: A wine with a pleasant level of acidity.

DRY: A wine that has no perceptible sweetness.

FAT: A full-bodied wine with little acidity.

FINISH: The aftertaste left by a wine.

FRUITY: The hint of fruit flavor evident in a wine.

GREEN: A wine that is too tart and acidic.

HARD: A wine with little fruit and too much tannin.

HEAVY: A robust wine in which the taste of alcohol is predominant.

LIGHT: A wine that has a light body and texture and is low in alcohol content.

LONG: An impressive, lingering aftertaste left by a wine.

OAKY: A woody flavor that results from aging a wine in oak casks or with oak chips.

PLONK: Derogatory term for a wine that is of undistinguished quality, i.e., a flop.

SOFT: A wine that leaves a smooth – not crisp – texture in your mouth.

SPICY: A term used to describe the aroma or scent of spices in a wine.

SWEETNESS: The sugar content of a wine, usually rated on a scale from zero (for very dry wines) to 10 (for very sweet wines, such as a Sauternes).

TANNIC: A red wine that leaves a sensation of dryness in your mouth.

We hope you enjoyed using *The Winemaker's Record Book*.

We welcome your comments and suggestions, and will incorporate the
best ideas into future editions. We will also send a complimentary copy
of the next edition to anyone who sends in a suggestion that we are
able to use. Address your comments to:

Project Editor
The Winemaker's Record Book
Raincoast Books
8680 Cambie Street
Vancouver, B.C.
Canada v6p 6m9